I0570757

PULLED OUT FOR A

PURPOSE:

Processed, Positioned, and Prepared

By Lorie Savage

Copyright© 2023 by Lorie Savage

All rights reserved.

First Edition, First Printing

No part of this book may be reproduced, stored in retrieval systems or transmitted in any form, by any means, including mechanical, electronic, photocopying, recording or otherwise, without prior permission of the publisher.

Printed in the United States of America

This book is dedicated to

My mother, Ann Hubbard; my children, Rodney Smith and

Alexis Savage; and my grandson, King Boyd.

Thank you for loving me through every season of my life!

With never-ending love,

Lorie Savage

Foreword

I am Dr. Dameion L. Royal, and I serve as the leading minister of both the Contending for the Faith Church in Wilson, North Carolina and the Philippi Church in Greenville, North Carolina. I first met the author nearly 20 years ago when she was beginning her formative years as a follower of Jesus Christ! I have had the honor of serving her in a pastoral capacity for nearly 12 years. During these years, I have been able to work closely with author and witness the wonderful ways in which God is working in her life! I welcome this new book which serves an awesome testament of salvation and hope. With over 30 years of fulltime ministry, I have seen lives that have been severely demolished due to a host of factors. People who find themselves in this state are often left feeling defeated and hopeless. Such feelings can cause individuals to be held hostage by guilt and shame. However, the testimony presented by this author serves as reminder that God can save anyone and give them a marvelous future! This work shows the reader that God's love for humanity knows no limits and that His grace can rescue mankind from the worst of places. The author of this book is Lorie Michelle Savage. She is a native of Greenville, North Carolina, and she serves as an associate minister of Philippi Church in Greenville. She is employed as Clinical Supervisor and Licensed Therapist, and she is the founder of Great Things Foundation which offers a variety of services intended to build the hope and esteem of women and girls. Under Lorie's leadership, the foundation has launched a host of mentoring events and support groups to build the lives of woman and girls, and as result, many individuals have been helped. Furthermore, Lorie consistently lends herself as an evangelist, conference speaker, and workshop facilitator. People near and far have been impacted by her ministry, and she continues to serve wherever she can make a difference. As Lorie has grown in the Lord, her light has been able to shine brightly before her family and friends. God has radically transformed her life in such a way that her ministry has gained the love, respect, and support of those closest to her. Among Lorie's greatest joy is that of being a mother and grandmother. She has a son, a daughter, a grandson, a sister, and a wonderful mother, all of whom she adores. Those who know her best celebrate her as a genuine and dedicated woman of God. Lorie is passionate about seeing lives transformed by the power of God, and her ministry reflects it. This fervor within her stems from her own transformational experience. She has endured deep drug addiction, alcoholism, relational abuse, promiscuity, and multiple forms of wayward living. Amazingly, she has experienced the deliverance of God in these areas. As her pastor, it has been awesome to witness the ways in which God has radically changed her life. My own life has been deeply inspired by hearing her testimony and witnessing how God continues to use her. She is the evidence of how God can take a life once riddled with defeat and do something dynamic with it! I am very confident that this book will bless the lives of those who read it. This text will give voice to Lorie's healing and deliverance journey. It is a powerful story of God's love, mercy, and redemption. While engaging this writing, the reader will be inspired and encouraged in a variety of ways. To those who continue to face the bondage of guilt and shame, this book will make it clear that freedom in Jesus is possible. This work will also be a powerful source of hope to those who have loved ones suffering from various forms of bondage and addiction. The author does an excellent job at reminding the reader that God can even redeem any life, even those which seem beyond repair. Read this book and allow it to bless your life! -Dr. Dameion L. Royal

TABLE OF CONTENTS

CHAPTER 1

Introducing My Journey:

My name is Lorie Michelle Savage, and I reside in Pitt County, North Carolina. I wish to share my journey with my readers, and it is my hope that you will be able to draw both inspiration and encouragement from it. To say the least, my life has been showered with an abundance of grace and mercy. I once felt like my life was hell on earth, but now it has amazingly changed for the better. Throughout the course of my life, I have faced many traumatic experiences. I was once haunted by alcoholism, severe drug addiction, domestic violence, rape, and so much more. Such experiences left me plagued by low self-esteem, rejection, guilt, shame, and abandonment! The direction of my life spiraled downward, and I eventually found myself in prison on an assault with a deadly weapon charge!

I wish to share how my life was able to rebound from a place of hopeless defeat to one of great victory! This is the story of a substance abuser who has now become a substance abuse therapist and clinical supervisor. I want to share my story of redemption. As a Born-Again disciple of Jesus Christ, I wish to tell my readers how I was given another chance at life! I seek to share how God took a life once defined by misery and

1

transformed it into one dedicated to ministry! It is my hope that those who follow my journey would emerge knowing that God can take a mess and turn it into a miracle. My life is the evidence, and it is with gratitude that I share my journey with you!

I hope to encourage my readers who may be on their own journey. I want everyone to know that irrespective of what that looks like, there is still hope. Whether you struggle with drug addiction, being unequally yoked with someone, not finishing school, or whatever the case may be, life does not have to end in these places. In fact, I have faced all these things, and by the grace of God, I have overcome them! Despite your struggle, you can still break free. You must not give yourself any excuses not to prevail.

This is my family who are a part of my story: My mom Annie, my dad James, my son Rodney, and my daughter Alexis. This is my story. This is their story. And this could very well be your story.

CHAPTER 2

Growing up in a dysfunctional home

I grew up on 4th Street, directly across from my elementary school, which was ironically called the Third Street School. We lived in a two-story apartment complex, and our two-bedroom apartment was on the second floor. My dad worked at Proctor and Gamble, and my mom worked at Cato's. My mom worked in retail for more than 35 years. She didn't have a driver's license, so she walked to and from work. Our apartment was not much, and we didn't have much. However, as dysfunctional as it was, it was full of love.

My mom had her first child at sixteen, and she felt that she missed out on her teenage years. Consequently, our house became known as the "party house." My mom drank alcohol and partied several times a week, especially on the weekends. My dad got paid every other Thursday, and I knew this because we were treated to McDonalds. By the time he came home, the records would be playing, and it would be the time for the parties. We always kept the latest albums and a comfortable sectional leather couch. Everyone would pile up at our house to get high, eat, sleep, and do whatever. During these times, I would get dressed up and put on a pair of my mom's high heel shoes. I would then sing Denise Williams songs, and I would go around drinking whatever was left in their cups. Amazingly, they didn't even notice. Everyone who attended the parties at my house seemed to be enjoying life and just having a good time. Little did I know that most of them were addicted to some mood-altering substance, and even my dad was a heroin user. People felt comfortable at our residence because my mom was always a giver to anyone in need, and she would open her house to anyone she could help.

When my grandma passed away, we moved into her house on Ward Street. It was "smack dab" in the middle of "the hood." We weren't exactly moving on up like the Jeffersons. Instead, we were moving kind of sideways. Ward Street was the "place to be." It was full of excitement, and there was always something going on. We were now living in a two-bedroom house in a central location which allowed us to do and see anything and everything. Everyone knew each other, and there were three clubs within walking distance. Sometimes, I would stick around without them knowing and "be grown up."

I remember my cousins living with us in that house, and we slept on the floor or anywhere we could find a spot. I was surrounded by love, and I was also surrounded by drugs and alcohol. There were clubs and liquor houses on every corner. Friday night, it was on. The drugs were attainable within six feet of the house, and we knew the families that sold them personally. Being the in "the hood" didn't take away from the community feel. On Ward Street, it wasn't unusual to hear anything alongside of the house, such as people using drugs, drinking on the back porch, or having sex. A host of things were going on. It ranged from witnessing shootouts to someone just sitting on the porch being entertained. It was nothing to see someone running through the yard trying to escape the police. There was a closeness among residents, but it was still so much dysfunction and chaos at the same time.

While growing up, one thing I remember is the string of broken promises from my father. I knew something was not right when we did not have heat at Christmas. I knew there was a problem if my dad said that radio player was in the shop, and then I would never see it again. I remember times that they said we would go to Disneyland and, of course, we never went. I think that's why I was so adamant about wanting to do things with my children. I wanted to go places and see new things with my kids because I grew up with so many broken promises. One Christmas season, my mom gave my dad money to get oil for the heater. It was almost Christmas, and we still had no heat because he used the money to get high. I remember that we rode around trying to get oil late at night. My mom was very upset, and they argued as I listened from the backseat. This was the moment that I started to realize that something was not right with my upbringing. Moreover, I started to notice when my dad and his friends went into his bedroom, seemingly doing fine, only to come back out high. I have memories of watching my cousins putting my dad in the tub and waking him up because he was overdosing. This happened more than once. I even remember my dad nodding off while driving, and the ashes of his cigarette would be so long because he would be too high to notice it. I now know that all his friends were addicts, and most of them died untimely and distasteful deaths. Many of them either overdosed, died from drug abuse complications, or succumbed to AIDS. My dad's health began to fail, and he continued to use substances despite his failing health.

As you can see, I grew up around difficult circumstances. It was a lot for a child to see, and it took a major toll on me. The dysfunction that I encountered in my youth left me feeling abandoned and opened the door for self-medication.

CHAPTER 3

My Experiences Getting High and Traumatic Rape

The first time I remember getting high, I was 5 years old. One of my mom and dad's friends would smoke a joint and blow the smoke in my face. As, I forestated, I would also drink any liquor leftover in their glasses and chug it down. By the time I was in middle school, I was pretty much a latch-key kid. My mom was busy working, and my dad was busy either working or boosting to support his heroin habit. I would ride my bike to the corner store and give a few dollars one of the alcoholics standing around to go in the store and buy me alcohol. They gladly did this for me. At that time, "Thunderbird" was my drink of choice. My paternal grandmother used to watch me, but at that time, it was not uncommon for kids my age to take their bikes and be gone all day. During this time, I did whatever. I would get myself a bottle and go to the park and drink my alcohol until I was drunk. Nevertheless, I always maintained enough sense to stay away from the adults when I came back. I never wanted them to notice that I was intoxicated.

By the time I was 15, I drank alcohol and smoked on a regular basis. As I approached high school years, I started experimenting with other drugs and snorting cocaine. I started smoking crack cocaine in the 11th grade. I first smoked crack cocaine with one of my close friends. She and I were dating two brothers, and we spent a lot of time together. She had already started smoking crack, and she even tried to deter me from doing it. At this time, I was already sniffing "coke," and my friend tried to warn me about how addictive crack cocaine was. Despite her warnings, I made the choice to smoke it anyway, and I thought it was the best thing in the world. The high was like five seconds, but I thought it was the best five seconds ever. Every part of my body was numb when I took a "hit." I felt great as I was able to escape reality for a moment.

My addiction caused my senior year in high school to become a blur. I do recall that I would go missing for a few days from school, but somehow, I always managed to keep up my schoolwork and my grades. Amazingly, I was able to graduate with no visible problems. However, I have no recollection of my graduation night because I was so intoxicated as I walked across the stage to receive my diploma. What should have been one of the most memorable nights of my life has escaped my memory due to my addiction.

By the time I finished high school, I was drinking alcohol, smoking marijuana, sniffing cocaine, and smoking crack cocaine. I was in full-blown addiction. Early on, I had plans to attend college, but my motivation to do anything productive decreased drastically. I talked my father into not forcing me to attend college immediately after graduating high school. I just told him to let sit out for about a year. That one year turned into 10 years, and it was 10 years of trauma, calamity, and turmoil.

At this time, I realized that I had lost control of my drug use, and I was at the point of no return. I was still dating my first love, and we both were addicted to crack. I was doing anything to keep up both of our habits, from stealing from my mother to smoking the entire drug dealer's package. I was in deep because I could have easily been killed for the latter. I felt like I was living in hell on earth and that there was no way out.

One morning, after I had done everything for us both to keep getting high the night before, my boyfriend looked at me and said, "You don't have any more money for us to get high?" At that very moment, I recall something hitting me like a ton of bricks! The thought that I was supporting the habit for myself and a man that was supposed to love me was too much, and that caused me to end my relationship with him. I did not want to be supporting a lazy man.

After separating myself from him, I went back on the westside, and I started hanging around my neighborhood and seeing what I could get into. Consequently, I began to "hang out" with my neighbor who lived across the street with his mother. He also kept "weed and coke," and I was sure to get high every time I saw him. After spending time with him, we started dating, although he was 13 years older me. In the beginning, everything was great until one horrible night. We were all hanging out with some of his friends. I thought everything was fine until he asked one of his friends to give us a ride to his sister's house. He seemed very agitated and annoyed at this time. When we arrived at his sister's house, she was not home, so he proceeded to break out her window to get into the house. At this moment, I did not know what to think because I had never seen him act this way. Once we got into the house, he hit me in my face with his fist. I was so shocked, and I thought that this could not be happening. He began to beat me like I was a man. He went on to hold me hostage, and he would not let me leave. He then made me have sex with him. I cannot even put into words how I felt.

The next day, he walked me home like nothing happened. When my mother saw me, she was in tears. I was almost unrecognizable as my swollen face was black and blue. I wish I could tell you that I left him after that, but I didn't, and the beatings got worse. The physical abuse was all based on him thinking that I was cheating on him or lying to him. The beatings escalated to a life-threatening level. One night, I was at a friend's house getting high as usual, and he was outside waiting in the bushes to attack me. He hit me in the head with a car jack and knocked me unconscious. He dragged me to his house and left me in the yard thinking I was dead. I was taken to the hospital, had part of my head shaved, and received seven staples in my head. That was a wake-up call for me. I ended that relationship by following the advice of his brother who told me that I should just leave him alone. I did just that!

Before I could leave, I conceived a child while in this relationship but had a miscarriage. I believe the miscarriage was a result of the beatings and trauma I suffered. Nevertheless, I know that the Lord does not make any mistakes, and He was watching over me even then. That same man is currently serving life without parole for killing his girlfriend in front of her daughter.

Well, at this point, I am single again and looking forward to my 21st birthday. For this celebration, we booked a suite at a hotel and had a cocaine party. I thought I was grown up. However, I was only grown up in legal age, but my decisions, thought patterns, and lifestyle reflected that of a 12- year-old. The party consisted of mostly males, all of whom enjoyed sniffing cocaine and drinking alcohol. I started dating my son's father around this time also. He was one of the guests at the party. The night was filled with indulging in drugs, alcohol, and "vibing" to the latest music by Monica, MC Lyte, Toni Braxton, DMX, and Snoop Dog! I thought it was a great night! I had all day to do what I wanted to do, which was to drink and smoke.

During this time, I did get a job at the Rubbermaid Plant, and I worked there for five years. I was a team leader, but my addiction took over and caused me to start getting high on the job. The plant administration was coming in one night to fire me. However, they couldn't find me because I was late coming into work. I knew they were coming to fire me, but I also knew if I told them I had a problem, they had to get me help. All the head people came to fire me, and I told them about my addiction. Further, I agreed to treatment. Not long after that the plant closed. They had to give me a severance package and unemployment. I had some money coming in, and I used it to get high. I was on welfare and getting a child support check for my son. It was $236 per month, and when I worked, I got paid weekly. All that money went to drugs. I was supporting my habit. I lied to my mom about needing money for things, I prostituted myself on the street, and I used my child support to support my habit. I got drugs any way I could. I just did not steal, but I would do anything else. All my morals and values went out the window. I had my son when I was 23.

During this time of intense addiction, I met a guy who I did not know. I knew his mom because she worked with me at

Rubbermaid. This guy seemed nice and gave me the impression that he was the "whole package." We went back to his house, and I got high there. He asked me about sex. He said, "I brought you here, you took my drinks and got high, so now it's time to pay up." He said that he was not going to take no for an answer. He raped me and took me back to where I was staying. It was humiliating. After this, I continued to get high so that I could forget it. It was a "date-rape" situation. The next time I saw this man, he was on the news for raping somebody. Apparently, he had done it before but never got caught. It was the "buzz" at Rubbermaid, and his mom knew everything.

Addiction was a major thing for me. It was a like a yearning in my belly that ran much deeper that a hunger for food. Addiction calls you. It calls you to that drug, and you cannot get rid of it. Once you get into that addiction, your mouth and nose are just above the water until the addiction pulls you down and you drown. Addiction is a nagging call that you cannot ignore. I had no power to resist it on my own. My whole existence centered around feeding my addiction. It had a powerful hold on me. Even when I was in rehab, I always felt the results of addiction. There was a taste in my mouth that kept me wanting beer or drugs all the time. I could go about three or four days, but then the cravings would get more and more intense, and I could not resist feeding them.

I would go two weeks at a time only feeding my addiction. I would binge, not bathing or seeing my family. While in this cycle, I would get enough nerve to go home and face my family. They never sought to reprimand me, and my mom was always glad to see me. She consistently welcomed me with open arms. I even recall one time that my mom thought I was dead. She sent one of my friends to look for me, and he found me and walked me home. He told me that my mom was worried, and when I arrived, she was sitting on the porch praying. When she saw me, she just asked me for a hug. Despite my mother's love, I continued to spiral downward in my addiction.

During this time, my family was relentless in wanting me to be free from my addiction. They even got together and brought loads of cars to the crack house, attempting to give me an intervention. The addicts in the house asked if that was my family. I said defiantly said, "I wish somebody would come and look for me." The truth is that I was trying to ignore it, but it was nine carloads of people hoping that I would want to come home. Instead, I was looking for the back door. That day, they brought my son out, and I behaved with great defiance. I acted like a "pure fool." I cussed everybody out that day. Looking back, I thank

God that my family loved me through my worse moments. I now realize that so many people don't have that support to recover. Addicts do not need to be surrounded by anyone giving judgment. My family was great during these moments. They loved me through my mess.

CHAPTER 4

My son's father, night of terror, and my son

After my 21st birthday, I was seeing more and more of a guy named Rodney. This guy had been trying to date me for years, as he and my last abusive boyfriend were friends. Rodney had a girlfriend at the time, which was cool with me because I was all about getting high and having fun. He would come to my house on every break from work, lunch break and every other break. He would also come to my house every night after work. We were together constantly. During this time, I did not smoke crack but was sniffing excessive amounts of cocaine. I started "catching feelings" for him and looked forward to seeing him and being with him. I became pregnant, which he was not happy about. He was already in a relationship, and I was what they call the "side piece." I had been with my first love for years and never used protection and never got pregnant. As forementioned, the next guy beat me so bad that I had a miscarriage. Honestly, I didn't think I could carry a child, and I had mixed emotions while I was pregnant. I always wanted a child but not like this. I was not that serious about this guy either. I had mixed emotions until I gave birth to my son.

I didn't believe in having an abortion, and I was determined to have my baby with or without him. At this time, he had started becoming verbally abusive. I started back smoking crack and would be missing for days at a time. I used drugs throughout my entire pregnancy. I would be in crack houses just thinking about everything I was consuming, and I could even feel my son moving in my stomach. However, I still could not beat this addiction. I prayed during my addiction asking God to help me, and my baby. I wanted God to save my baby because it was not his fault. I prayed that he would have a fighting chance.

I went into labor at the neighborhood corner store. During delivery, as my son was being born, he was not crying nor was he breathing. However, my aunt was in the delivery room with me. All she could do was look into my eyes with love and assure me that everything was going to be alright. After what seemed like hours, I finally heard my son cry! Jesus is so wonderful! My son was born on May 19, 1995. I prayed that my baby would live, and he did. He weighed 5 pounds 8 ounces. He was everybody's favorite. He had these really big eyes that tugged at your heart. His dad started acting like a "proud father" at this time. People were telling my sons paternal grandfather that they had a grandchild, and they wanted to meet him. His dad took him meet them, and they became inseparable. They loved him from the moment they laid eyes on him. They were very supportive and treated him like a little prince.

I thought the birth of my son would be my motivation to give up drugs and the lifestyle that came along with it. I was doing good for about nine months and having a decrease in my usage. Around February 1996, I was living in a one-bedroom apartment with my new baby and his dad. My son was 9 months old at that time. His dad and I continued to have issues, and we argued all the time. Before going home one night, we were drinking and smoking marijuana. I had gone to my mother's house, and she asked me not to go home this specific night. She asked me to stay with her. However, I packed up with my baby and his dad, and we proceeded to our apartment. When we arrived home, I realized that our phone and cable had been cut off, and I could not understand why. At his request, I did not work. He expressed that he would provide for me and my son. I began looking through his checkbook, and I saw that he had written checks to his daughter's mother. I did not have a problem with this; I had a problem with things not being taken care of in our home. When I asked him about it, he became very defensive and verbally abusive. I think I had a flashback of the past abuse I had endured. I went and got a knife, and he got a broom. I stabbed him in the heart. I wanted to hurt him but never intended to stab him in the heart. I sat down and continued to drink alcohol. He went into the bathroom and pulled the knife out and when he did, blood was everywhere, even coming out of his mouth. At this time, I finally realized that I had seriously hurt him. After finally realizing that this situation had seriously escalated, I ran and knocked on several apartment doors trying to get help. I knew that time was of the essence now and began to panic. Because I was covered in blood, looking like someone out of a horror movie, no one would open their doors to help me. I gave up and went back to the apartment to see what I could do. As soon as I arrived at the house, a man, who was dressed in white appeared at the door and went to get help. I choose to believe that he was an angel sent by God because he saved Rodney's life. Everything moved so quickly; my baby was still in the car seat. I was not a good housekeeper, and my house had bottles everywhere. I was sitting down drinking and my baby was asleep in the car seat while all this happened. Things escalated so quickly. When I looked up again, the police were outside the door with the coroner. They did not know if Rodney was dead or alive. Moreover, all the local news reporters started arriving. I asked if I could ride with him in the ambulance, and they told me, "Ma'am he is going in the red and white and you are going in this blue and white." They told me that I needed to call someone to come and get my son or they would find a placement for him. It didn't hit me as to what I had done until I woke up the next day on a cold, hard concrete floor inside of a jail cell.

My aunt who lived in New York came to be with me, as I was going to have my first court appearance. During this time, Rodney was having open-heart surgery from the stabbing and was unable to talk to the officers. I was initially charged with attempted murder. When Rodney came out of surgery, he was able to tell them what happened. At this point, the charge was reduced to assault with a deadly weapon inflicting serious injury. When I made bail, I went home and continued to drink alcohol and get high, knowing that I almost took someone's life.

I can remember a great friend of the family heard what happened and came to just sit with me. She did not talk, she didn't pass judgment, but she was just there to sit with me. That was the first time I was made aware of the power of someone's presence. That was the first time that I realized that silence could be such an effective response. Until this very day, I'm grateful for her showing me love and support in such an unconventional way.

Once my son's father gained consciousness, he kept sending word through my father that he wanted to see me. My dad said, "Mickey, you need to see him. He is asking for you." I was hesitant to go because I didn't know what to expect, and I could not understand why he would want to see me after what I had done. After arriving at the hospital, I remember my son's father saying to me, "Look what you did to me. I love you, now give me a kiss!" He smelled the alcohol on me and asked how I could continue drinking after what had happened. I had no words.

I went to court in May 1996, and I was to appear in Superior Court. During the trial, Rodney asked to testify in my defense. He told the judge that I was the mother of his child and that he just wanted me to get help and treatment. He pleaded with the judge not to send me to prison. As a matter of fact, he made the front page of the newspaper that day and the headline read "Man Does Not Want Girlfriend to Go to Jail Because He Loves Her." After his testimony, my charges were reduced to assault with a deadly weapon. He was very instrumental in my case. Rodney still has plates in his chest until this day due to almost losing his life. I also had several family members who were character witnesses. People were able to identify the addiction and not attack my character. What I needed was treatment. I have learned that addicts need someone can discern who they really are void of substances, environment, situations, or circumstances. The sentence I received was six months in prison, and I was ordered complete drug and alcohol recovery treatment. I would be under intensive probation when I returned home.

When I returned home, addiction overtook me again. I had series of probation violations that resulted in several stays in jail. Thus, my son was raised primarily by his paternal grandparents. His grandparents were educators and had more than I could ever give him at that point. I kept him on the weekends and tried to be a good mother.

When my son was growing up, he couldn't stand loud noises. He had to have a routine, and he hated change. He was very angry during this time, as he did not understand why he could not stay with me and was living with his grandparents. He thought it was because he was "bad." I assured him that it was not him. I was sick and needed help. When I came home from prison, he was excited to see me. It didn't matter what bad things I did, he loved his mommy. However, I was still sick and desired the drugs more than I desired my children at this point.

I remember one day that it seemed like the drugs were calling my name. I tried to get out of the house before he saw me. But he kept his eyes on me, as if he knew I would try to leave him. I attempted to sneak away but he saw me. He cried and tried to hold on to me, but I wanted to be in the streets more. The vision of him crying for me still haunts me to this very day.

After continuing with my addiction and being in and out jail, my relationship with my son's dad was totally dismantled. He tried to salvage the relationship, but I was just not stable enough to maintain it. Thankfully, He and I are on good terms now. He even calls me for prayer and advice, and I can even help to calm him down at times. I thank God for this!

CHAPTER 5

My Prison Experience and Release

At my original sentencing, I was given probation for six months. It was an intensive probation that required me to remain clean and sober for six months and submit to a 6 p.m. curfew daily. I was only able to comply with this probation for maybe a month or two. When I violated probation the first time, I was sent to prison to await trial for my probation violation. The judge sentenced me to six months in prison. When I returned home, I was to go back on supervised probation for another six months. Throughout this ordeal, I was arrested on several occasions for probation violation such as missing curfew and positive drug screens. When my son was about 2 years old, I violated my probation and was sent to jail again. At this time, I found out I was pregnant with my daughter.

Once the state discovered that I was pregnant, they immediately let me out on probation. The state did not want to be responsible for a pregnant woman. This time I was sent home with an "ankle bracelet." This device was a GPS that would monitor my location constantly. I did well for a month or so, but I started using drugs again. I did not care about carrying a baby or the ankle bracelet. I was arrested and went to jail, and by this time I was eight months' pregnant, I told my probation officer that I wanted to complete my entire sentence. I wanted to do the 16 months in prison, in hopes of obtaining recovery. I just got tired. I was desperate to get clean and have a life free of drugs and alcohol.

I was sentenced to 16 months in the state prison. It was the 27th of May 1998, and I was admitted to the state prison. I did not know what it would be like. I was unsure as to what was going to happen. My initial concern was who would keep my child because we would be separated at her birth. I had my daughter the day after I was admitted to prison! I was shackled and chained to a bed at Wake Med Hospital in Raleigh, NC. When you are a ward of the state, you are not allowed to keep your baby with you. If you do not have a family member or someone to place your child with, the Department of Social Services will place them in foster care without the guarantee of you reuniting with your child once you are released. Thankfully, I had parents who would not have it any other way than to care for their newborn granddaughter. I called my mom and dad to come and get her. I had to sign over guardianship of my daughter to them knowing that she would be loved and cared for until I completed my sentence of 16 months. After my daughter was born, I had one day to bond with my daughter. The next day, I was transported back to the prison to finish my sentence.

I did not get to see my mom or daughter much because my mom did not drive or have license. For the next 16 months, prison would be my home. I resided in a quad that could be likened to a dorm. It was 30 to 40 women in the quad. When you enter prison, your life is not your own. Permission must be granted for everything that you do. You must be accounted for every hour of the day. They call it "count time." During this time, you are to stop whatever you are doing and remain where you are to be accounted for. This is to ensure no escapes and the safety of all individuals. Many of the ladies go out from the quad for jobs, and no one could sign in or out without permission. It was a highly structured environment.

During this time, if I was not out, I got to sit on my bunk and reflect on my life. I also had time to meditate on God's word, allow Him to speak to me, my situation, and give me instructions on how to live. I was given an Amplified Bible at one of the church services. I studied that Bible and stood on the promises of God. Reading God's Word became a safe place for me. Prison had a lot of dangerous things, and I needed a spiritual road map on how to make it home safely.

There were drugs in the prison as well. Everything that you could get on the outside, you could get on the inside of prison. Nevertheless, it was a place where I needed to be at that time in my life. Do not get me wrong, I just simply believe that all things work together for the good of those who love the Lord. Prison was like a little town inside of Raleigh. You have all kinds of women-- short women, tall women, small, big, round, long, evil, and loving women. I took upholstery, nail tech, culinary arts classes, and anything else I could think of to stay away from trouble. Trouble seemed to be everywhere. It felt like I was in a war zone, but I was being divinely protected by God. I signed up for every church service that preached Jesus.

The outside world would never believe what happens behind the prison walls. Homosexuality is in there. There were females who look just like men! I was approached by a woman wanting a relationship with me. At first, I was trying to be nice but quickly realized that I needed to shut this thing down. I was a distraction from the enemy and could very well lead to my demise. I drew the line, and she learned quickly what my life was about. It is easy to be pulled into a pit with no way out. I knew I had to make it out alive. This was something that I dabbled in during my addiction. It wasn't who I was, but it came along with the lifestyle.

Prison can really be the devil's playground. I can remember being told that this girl was a snitch who was housed in the same quad. One night, some of the inmates tied locks in towels and beat her so bad that she had to be transported to another prison for "safe keeping." One young girl had seizures and just died. She was very young, so I believe it was because of the medical attention. I have seen women die in prison and never make it home.

I was able to leave the prison during the day to work because of good behavior. I worked for a dollar a day at a café that served prison staff. Some inmates would find ways to break the rules. While working, male inmates would come and deliver produce or meat. Some of the women inmates would go in the freezer to have sex at that risk of getting an STD, getting pregnant, solitary confinement, or losing all privileges. I was exposed to many things but never allowed anything to distract me from making it home. My thought was to get through it and just survive. Their motto was, "What's done in there stays in there." I didn't want to be a statistic or to have to battle any extra demons. I focused on building up my spiritual and physical body. I worked out with an inmate named Eugenia who was my friend. We worked out, walked, ran, and tried to support each other mentally and emotionally. We talked about what brought us there and what we would do when we returned home.

That place was full of wickedness, and the presence of evil could be felt there. The smell was dark and gloomy. It was like a dungeon. My children and family were on the outside, and I needed to get back to them. While I was there, I prayed and prayed more than I have ever prayed before. I had to make the best of it. I just wanted to get home and get out alive. Prison life was never for me. I simply was not cut out for it and would never get used to it. My addiction drove me to that life of despair, desperation, and dysfunction.

I went through a program called DART (Drug Alcohol Recovery Treatment) while in prison, as it was a requirement of my sentence. As part of DART, we lived in a separate quad that was specifically for those going through this 90-day program. I was appointed inmate drug counselor of our quad. I was in charge of other inmates living in the quad who had substance use issues. I made sure they did their chores, followed quad rules, and cleaned the dorm. That was part of my job duties. I also was available to counsel them on any recovery issues.

While I was in prison, I had to ask myself about what I wanted my life to be. I had two children back at home. As much as I hated it, prison in a way was my safe place. I was grateful for it. It was a rescue mission for me. It was a foundation for me to try to get grounded and secure in God. One of the greatest things that happened to me in prison was to receive a Bible. I wanted to do all I could to learn about Jesus and His ways. I believe it was what could help me with this demon of addiction.

My prison number was 0533483. We had to know our number, as it was how we were identified in prison. We wore brown clothes in reception and blue clothes in medium security. Green clothing was for minimum security. The minimum security had more freedom and better food. We ate well. Yellow uniforms were for the death row inmates. Orange clothing meant you were long-term inmates or lifers. We had to pass the death row inmates to go to church. I remember during my prison time there was a prisoner, Blanche Kiser Taylor Moore, who was known as the "Black Widow." She was a serial killer. She poisoned her boyfriend and others close to her. Well, we were all in prison together. She had a book and a movie about her life, so she thought she was a star. One inmate was especially weird. Apparently, she was married and had a baby and the husband loved the baby so much that she killed the baby and fed it to her husband. I saw her often. There were several women in there from my hometown whom I knew but they looked totally different in prison. It was as if they were living a different life now. Some of the best singers in the world were in there, anointed voices. That was my first lesson in learning the difference between a gift and the anointing. There were women who could sing like nothing you have ever heard, but they detested the name of Jesus. There were ladies from all walks of life in prison.

There was witchcraft and all sorts of evil on those grounds. I was determined to look straight ahead, stay focused, and keep going. There were women there who would never go home. They would see people come and go and the year on the calendars just changed. There were some good people in prison, too, like the young lady who did my hair every two weeks. She taught me the "dos and don'ts" of prison life. She had been there a long time and was from Greensboro, NC. We both cried when it was her time to be discharged. I can remember one inmate who had been there for 24 years. She killed her boyfriend, and she knew she'd be there the rest of her life. It was so much to take in and so many different people, and I really didn't know who to trust.

The worst part for me was not being able to call home or to see my family often. Visitation was on Saturday and Sundays based on your last name. My visitation day was Sunday. We would get "made up" and have our hair done on visiting days. But if I prepared and they could not make it, that was a big disappointment to me. I remember holidays and especially Christmas being in prison. It was a very sad and lonely time. But these were the consequences of the choices that I made. We had to be stripped-searched after every visit. It was hard knowing that I couldn't leave with them when they visited. It was just heart-breaking. There's nothing I could do about it but cry and hope for brighter days.

I was in the Raleigh Corrections Center for Women first, and then the North Carolina Correctional Institution for Women. Lastly, I was moved to minimum security prison on State Street where I did most of my sentence.

When it was time for me to be released. I had already talked with my case manager and was scheduled to leave. I packed all week, but I had many things going through my mind. I could feel fear taking over my being. I thought about the real world. I was isolated in prison, and thus, it was easy to stay clean and sober. I was preparing to go home, but I was consumed with concerns of how my life would be. I was excited that I was leaving with tools to maintain sobriety, but I was still afraid to go home. I knew what my life was like before I was sentenced to prison, and I knew what my surroundings would be when I returned home.

My daughter's father visited me in prison, and he told me that he would make sure I got whatever I needed when I returned home. I was drawn to that and the lifestyle. I was drawn to the sex we had and that we would have when I returned home. It was a one-way ticket from the devil to destroy my life. That was indeed a soul tie that I knew I needed to break away from, but it would not happen right away.

I was released on parole, and my parole officer picked me up and transported me to Greenville where I would try to stay out of prison and hopefully continue in sobriety. When I returned home in 1999, I knew that people would come from far and near. However, I was not sure if I would be strong enough to stay away from trouble. I had to stay busy and keep working. I knew if I had idle time and nothing to do, I would fall back to doing what was familiar. I needed to sustain and maintain the healthy lifestyle I had made a habit of. I knew I had to get a job, and by the grace of God, I found employment with benefits. I did well for a while. However, about six months later, I started using again and in 2002. I almost lost my life, and this was the final countdown for me.

CHAPTER 6

Freedom From Addiction

Addiction is so powerful. I would not want anyone to go through the agony and dependence that drug use brings. Many do not make it out of this struggle alive, so I am forever grateful. Nobody wakes up and says that they want to be a crack addict when they grow up. It was hell on earth for me. I would sometimes go up to two weeks at a time with no bath, no food, only surviving on drugs. I even set my hair on fire trying to smoke crack! I just wanted to be high. I found myself in places I never imagined myself being. It was a very low time for me.

I tried rehab and different locations, but it was Jesus who delivered me. The night I was delivered, I will never forget it. I had been out on a binge, and I saw a guy that I met a week before. I had not seen him for a few days, and I brought him to my friend's house. When my friend saw him, he immediately said that he was not allowed in his house. I was intentional about getting high, and I was going to do so by any means necessary. So, we left there and headed to Thomas Foreman Park and sat in the dugout. I was excited as I knew I was about to indulge in crack-smoking. I believed that he had the "package," and I had the paraphernalia.

To fully understand that God was with me, let me explain something. A few weeks beforehand, I had fallen and broken my arm and never went to get medical treatment. While in the dugout, without warning, this guy reached over and started choking me. He did not say anything. He did not beat me. He did not try to rape me. His only intention was to try to take my life. It was around 3 a.m. and no one knew where I was. I couldn't holler for help because he had his arm wrapped around my neck. As I struggled with one good arm and a crack pipe in the other, I realized that I was about to die. I thought that I was on my way to hell with a crack pipe in my hand! I prayed to God and asked Him to spare my life, and I promised God I would walk away from drugs forever.

Somehow, I was able to scream, "Jesus!" and every time I would call on that GREAT NAME, He would back up. I kept right on yelling, "Jesus!" I called the Name of Jesus two more times. Because there is power in that Name, I witnessed that devil back up enough for me to run for my life! I wear glasses but they were knocked off during the shuffle. I could not really see (being legally blind in my right eye). Nevertheless, I was able to see a yellow bar and some lights from the street that guided me to the highway. Supernatural strength took over, and I was able to jump the fence with my broken arm. I waved down a car on Memorial

Drive that was driven by a nurse. She took me to the hospital, and I was hollering "Jesus" the whole time. The Lord had answered my prayer and spared my life!

A few days later, this guy walks across the yard of my mother's house. I'm not sure if he knew I lived there, but I was scared to death and called the police. They were able to question him and ask for his identification and assured me they would take care of it. The next week that same man killed two women, one he strangled, one he stabbed, burned, and tried to bury her. He tried to hide out in Raleigh with his family, but once they saw him on the news and what he had done, a family member turned him in.

This same man killed two women, and I would have been the first victim BUT FOR THE GRACE GOD! I was no different from the other ladies. The devil was trying to make me the first one. God rescued me in a way that no one else could ever get the credit for. I would have been his first victim, but I was PULLED OUT FOR A PURPOSE.

By God's Grace, I gave Jesus my life on February 1, 2002. I knew quite well that I should be silenced by death, but the Lord spared my life. His Grace and Mercy brought me through. The songwriter said, "I'm living this moment because of God!" Again, this man did not try to rape me, but he was sent straight from the pit of hell just to KILL me. He did not beat me up, but

36

his assignment was to kill me. The enemy comes to kill, steal, and destroy. But Jesus came that we might have abundant life. God said, "You're going to live for Me." My testimony is clear: I HAVE BEEN PULLED OUT FOR A PURPOSE!

CHAPTER 7

Saved, But Unequally Yoked

Well despite my being saved, I started as a definite "babe in Christ." When I returned home from prison, my daughter, who I had given birth to there, was a toddler, and she was walking and talking. Also, my son was 3 years old. I wanted very much to serve Jesus the best I knew how, and I was making strides to do everything I thought was right. I maintained a strong connection with my daughter's father during this time. He was about 20 years older. I had always known him and his family. I was selling cocaine at one point, and he was a regular customer before I became my own BIGGEST customer. When I started dating him, I was pregnant with my son. I was out walking late one night, and he drove by and asked me if I wanted a ride. He seemed shocked to know that I was pregnant and out walking so late at night.

We were not intimate initially, but we became very close after my son was born. We would "hang out" and spend lots of time together. We became inseparable. Neither one of us called it dating, however. He was my "sugar daddy" and supplied me with money and drugs at the time. After giving birth to my son, we took our relationship to another level. We started hanging out more and doing whatever came to our imagination.

A few years later I became pregnant with our daughter. It was foggy because I was high. I got hooked on my own supply. Biggie was right: "Don't get hooked on your own supply." I was going back and forth to New York City and brought the drugs back here. Even though there was a big age difference, I liked how he treated me. He was chivalrous, kind, and complimented me daily. He would send me flowers and leave me love notes. These things made me feel special.

I was heavy in my drug addiction and would still see my son's father "off and on." After I gave God my life in 2002, conviction started getting the best of me. I was consistently sleeping with my daughter's father, and we were not married. I didn't want to live like that anymore. I was tired of "laying up" in the hotel on Saturday night and singing in the choir on Sunday morning. There was no pomp and circumstance; he did not propose or get on one knee. I just went home and told him that if we were going to continue seeing each other, we needed to be married. He agreed, and we were married in 2004. We had a long and very dysfunctional relationship. There was constant arguing, and he was still using drugs although I was no longer into the lifestyle. By this time, I had absolutely no desire of returning to it.

Now I understand why the Bible specifically says, "Do not be yoked together with unbelievers. For what do righteousness and wickedness have in common? Or what fellowship can light have with darkness? What harmony is there between Christ and Belial? Or what does a believer have in common with an unbeliever?" (2 Cor. 6:14-15). I always knew he was not right for me, and I always had the notion that I was only marrying because I could not control my flesh. I felt that I could further pacify my flesh in the confines of marriage. I was not attracted to him, but I did love him. For me, his attention was appealing.

The marriage was not good. He said he was saved, but his lifestyle did not match what his mouth was saying. He went to church when he wanted to make things right. He hung out with guys all night. He would not come home until late at night. He would not socialize with my friends or engage in anything with anyone other than "his boys." He did not want my friends to know who he really was. He would not come out of his room if people came over, and my friends would say that he was not supportive. They would often say, "Why are you with him? It's not a good fit." Although we were married in 2004, he was not what God intended for my life.

Now, I realize that I am a servant of God, and I can tell others not to sell themselves short or have a blind eye when it comes to the things that the enemy sends to distract and detour us. The person you join yourself to in marriage matters.

CHAPTER 8

Dealing with My Daughter's Sex Abuse

Being married to my daughter's father welcomed many problems to my life. However, I could have never imagined what having him in our house would cost my family. I will never forget one of the most devastating days of my life. I was attending a women's conference at my church. The guest speaker encouraged us to close our eyes and just focus on the Lord and His goodness. After the service, one of my sisters in Christ came to me and said that sometimes children go through things that they are unable to share with their parents, like when someone is touching them inappropriately. She used herself as an example, and then she just began to hug me.

I knew at that very moment that someone had been molesting my daughter, and I just hollered from my belly at the mere thought of someone doing that to her. I went to my car and called a friend to try to process it all. I called a parent of one of my daughter's friends to see if she had told her anything. She told me that my daughter said it was her father who was molesting her. I got in my car to go to where my daughter was. I asked her if this was true, and she confirmed that her father was sexually abusing her.

I took her to the hospital to be examined, and then I called the police to have him arrested.

After making sure my daughter was safe, I got in my car and was headed to where he was. I had made up my mind that I was going to hurt him for what he had done. Halfway there, the Holy Spirit said, "Turn the car around and go home. Vengeance is mine. I will take care of it." I turned the car around and went home, trusting God. She was only 14 years old when we found out about the abuse. She stated that she could not remember how long it had been going on, as she tried to block out the painful memories. She had written in her diary and drew pictures about what he had been doing to her. Although the evidence from the doctor could not definitively detect my daughter's ongoing sexual abuse, I knew that she was telling the truth. I immediately had her number changed and his phone disconnected from our family plan. After her dad heard that this had gotten out, he was constantly trying to call her to convince her that her assault did not happen.

By this time the police were at his job questioning him and, of course, he denied it. I had his clothes and belongings taken to his friend's house, and I had all the locks of the house changed. My main objective was to ensure that my daughter was safe. During the investigation, my daughter was questioned at her school by an investigator without my permission. She questioned my daughter at a place that her peers attended. I am sure my daughter was embarrassed and was still trying to understand it all. My daughter recanted her story and said that her father never touched her. I believe that she just wanted it over. Also, she had mixed feelings of trying to understand how someone she loved could do something so horrible to her. It was just so overwhelming for her. Nevertheless, no charges were brought against him.

After the trauma of sexual assault, my daughter and I were left trying to pick up the pieces. I felt like our lives had been shattered into a thousand little pieces. My daughter went to therapy and refused to talk to the therapist. At this time and during the times of her abuse, I believe she wanted to end her life.

I began to connect the dots concerning things I had wondered about. For some time, I could see where my daughter had cut the screen out of her bedroom window either to escape from her dad or run from the pain she was suffering. There were times when she would come into my bedroom and just sleep on the floor. This didn't seem out of the ordinary to me because they always liked sleeping on the floor. She would ask to stay at my mom's house and would cry if she could not. I now know and understand that she was trying to get away from her father. She trusted some people in church but was not able to "open up" to them. She did not want to talk about it with anyone. She referred to her journal and was able to express her feelings through her writings. The police kept it for evidence. They would not arrest him. They stated that it was her word against his. Who can really comprehend why a father would do such a thing to his own daughter?

Now that my daughter's father was out of the house, she finally felt secure and safe. Sometime later, we were at church, and my daughter was in a group with teenagers. She was talking or doing something that caused one of the church leaders to correct her. My daughter did not like this, and she started to use her abuse as an excuse for her behavior. She decided to walk from church to the magistrate's office. I was told by the officer that as soon as she arrived, she screamed, "My father raped me!" The officer told me that the case would have to be reopened, and they would be glad to do so. However, my daughter was against it. Again, her father was never charged for his crimes.

One of the biggest tricks of the enemy is to try to make you think that God does not love you. If he can deceive us about this, we are done. By God's Grace, I held on to what I knew! I was persuaded that no matter what comes, no matter how painful, God loves me. I was reminded of one of the many lessons my pastor, Dr. Dameion Royal, taught me, "The devil is no opposite equal to God." Instead, the devil is a created being, and can never be greater than God, our Eternal Creator. Our pastor often reminds us that God is not the cause of everything that happens in our lives, but he can surely use everything that happens in our lives. We are constantly reminded that no moment with God is wasted. Even the seasons we do not prefer, God can use them to form something precious in our lives! These things settled it for me! I realized that God didn't cause this terrible thing to happen, but He could use these moments to bring forth something beautiful. God is still at work doing just that.

As for my ex-husband, I forgave him, but it took a while. I wanted him to hurt like I and my daughter hurt. Nevertheless, I asked the Lord to help me. In response, He healed my heart. I now pray for his deliverance. We separated in 2012 and were divorced in 2013.

CHAPTER 9

Mending the Relationship with My Daughter

My relationship with my daughter has always been somewhat strained. As I previously stated, my daughter was born the day after I arrived in prison. When I returned home, she was 18 months old. During this time, I was still using drugs. Even after I came home, for a while, I was never present. This caused our relationship to suffer from the start. When I began to turn my life around, I was busy in school or working trying to make a better life for myself and my children. I was determined that they would never take the road that I did or engage that negative lifestyle. By the grace of God, I assumed responsibility for my daughter. Because I wanted better for my children, I was strict with her. I was learning how to be a good parent. I was used to parenting being "high." However, parenting while being sober is much different.

The incident with her dad was a dividing line between my daughter and me. I feel in my heart that if I had just come upstairs at the time, I would have known. My daughter mentions that I did not go upstairs. "If you had only come upstairs," she always says. She always felt unsafe upstairs, and one of the things a parent is supposed to do is to keep their child safe. This truly has caused another divide in our relationship.

After my daughter's abuse, we had a challenging time. She wanted to go with her friends, stay out all night, and she would often bring up the abuse in the process. I was determined to have order and respect in my home. I was not going to continue to allow the enemy to have his way in my house or any part of our lives. Prayer has always been a part of my walk with God, and I had to turn it up a notch during this trying time.

I realized the whole matter of my daughter's abuse left me depressed. I was taunted by the enemy day and night. I am a therapist by training, and I see abusive behavior daily in my line of work. I questioned myself as to why I did not see any of the signs about my daughter's abuse. Guilt, shame, and worthlessness was all that I felt. This ordeal was a devastating time for my daughter. It was extremely difficult for me as well. However, we made it through with help of God.

Despite her challenges, my daughter has emerged from the ashes victoriously. She is making great progress and becoming a remarkable young woman in many ways! God has showered her life with grace, and I am proud of her. With the help of God, my daughter has been empowered through her pain. She has created a YouTube channel to encourage other young girls with her story.

I am forever grateful to God for allowing us to move forward through our pain.

My daughter and I still have work to do, but I do know that she loves me. When I was admitted to the hospital due to sickness, she was there around the clock. I stayed a week and had to go back immediately after I was discharged. She was committed to being by my side throughout this ordeal. My heart was delighted that she was there for me in that way.

My daughter is now the mother to a beautiful son. When she was pregnant, our relationship got even stronger. I am glad to report that we are doing better than we ever have. We talk daily now, and I am happy. We are making strides in our relationship and looking to Jesus to heal every broken place.

CHAPTER 10

Breaking the Cycle of Addiction

Do not experiment with drugs; it is playing with fire. I started as a child with a mind not fully developed yet. Alcohol or marijuana--don't even try it, as you will have no control once you are addicted. Addiction is dangerous and deadly. Run from substance abuse, and do not even think about it. It is far too costly. It can rob you of your future, and in many cases, your life. My story is one of just a few that made it out alive. Like many people, I thought, "I got this." The truth is that the drugs had me. Stay away from drugs. This is my initial advice.

Nevertheless, those who are fighting against addiction need learn to manage your emotions. This means that you need to identify with what you are feeling, and deal with it in healthy ways. I recommend engaging in extracurricular activities. They keep you busy. Link up with positive people and find a safe place to express yourself. Having a safe outlet like journaling, writing, and singing has helped me to maintain a healthy lifestyle.

Most of all, those fighting against addiction must allow God to be their source for everything! A lot of times when we go through things like addiction, our past causes guilt, shame, and fear. It takes the help of God to overcome that. Attending church and having a personal relationship with God through Jesus Christ tremendously helped me. Cry out to God and ask for His help. He wants to rescue you! Get in a good Bible teaching church. Learn God's Word and apply it. Serve in a local church as it is appropriate and connect with other believers in Christ who can strengthen you. Serving other people gives me great joy, and it has helped me in indescribable ways. Outreach ministry and giving back has been a great part of my life and my recovery!

Also, find your true identity in Jesus Christ. The devil and the world will try to limit who you are, but they don't define you. You are defined by your creator, Jesus Christ. Even when I first came to the church, some people still identified me as "the girl from the streets." They did not realize that the streets were where I came from but not who I am. Furthermore, my addiction had defined my life for many years, but I learned that my real definition came from God. You need to know who you are through God's Word. For a long-time I was called bum, slut, and crack head. Nevertheless, I had to believe more about what God said concerning my identity. I am a new creation in Christ! My sins have been forgiven, and my past has been covered. I have been accepted into God's beloved! I am a son of God! This is not just true of me; it is true of everyone who gives their life to Jesus Christ!

Moreover, I learned that deliverance is an everyday decision. Daily, I had to be determined and relentless in progressing in Christ and taking my life back. I had to keep going no matter what came at me. I had to develop a made-up mind. If I did not keep going, I would end up back in the streets or dead. I was determined not to give the devil that chance.

If you want to win the fight, it will take depending on the strength of God and surrounding yourself with people who care about you. Without question, you need a strong support system. Thankfully, I had a very supportive family. This helped me tremendously. We may say that we don't need anyone, but we all need someone. I had no clothes and no car; I had nothing of my own. My mom gave me her clothes to wear to church. I caught rides until I was able to get a car of my own.

Those who are fighting addiction need to find someone whom to be accountable. We all need people who we will allow to be honest with us. I was helped by being around people like this. They help you to become successful.

Furthermore, if you want to make progress. set goals for yourself Start out with easily attainable goals and make the necessary steps to accomplish them. Get in school and improve your circumstances one step at a time. Work hard and strive for something meaningful. It will keep you from relapsing.

When I realized that I could achieve things, I expanded my goals. I started to achieve my goals. I always wanted to attend college but because of my addiction, I just did not think it was possible. After a year in recovery, my brother-in-law, Jeff Savage was working at Shaw University at the time. I expressed my interest in going to college. He told me that if I would take the first step in completing the application, he would help me in any way he could. Graduating college was one of the greatest achievements in my life.

Philippians 4:13 (my favorite Scripture) in the Bible says that "I can do all things through Christ who strengthens me," and to this day I've been clean for over 20 years. I can't believe it myself. I always thought I would be addicted. I never thought it was possible when I was addicted. I never imagined being clean. It blows my mind. It was addiction or death. I did not think I could stop it. It was too powerful for me to stop. I couldn't control it. My life centered around it. It was such a strong hold on me.

I constantly prayed to God about never returning to addiction. One morning I awakened realizing that the urge was gone. I was in awe of God! A month had passed, and I still had no desire or urge to get high! I was like, "WOW, I'm really in recovery!" The urges and cravings were all gone! My freedom from addiction has been priceless! I am fully persuaded that God holds all power! God did it for me! In the past, I had tried everything. I tried therapy, I tried AA, and I was in inpatient treatment a few times. I tried nearly everything available and still could not get free my addiction. The power of God did not disappoint. He pulled me out just when I needed it the most. No more butterflies in my stomach, and after that day, I determined that I was a walking miracle.

CHAPTER 11

Manifesting your Divine Purpose

I want readers to gain insight into their own lives through this book. I want them to know that they can achieve anything, and I pray that this reading offers hope and strength. We all get in situations that seem hopeless, and we often think that we cannot emerge from this place. Nevertheless, by the help of God, we can make it. There was a time when I felt hopeless, and I thought I would always be a drug addict. If I can do it, surely you can also. I'm not a superhero, but I serve an Undefeated Champion who can help you win in every season of your life. I just thank God for His grace that was extended toward me. GOD PULLED ME OUT FOR A PURPOSE! God will do the same for you!

Today, I stand as a living testimony of God's Greatness! My heart is full of gratitude and my mouth sings forth with praise! The Lord has been very kind to me! HE PULLED ME OUT FOR A PURPOSE. I started out battling addiction, and my life spiraled almost to death. At one point, I lived in defeat and shame. I am glad to report that this is no longer my story. By the grace of God, I was PULLED OUT FOR A PURPOSE!

Today, I can report that God has done amazing things in and through my life! I stand firmly as a Born-Again disciple of Jesus Christ. For over twenty years, God has allowed me to grow in the grace and knowledge of who He is. After years of being bound in a mess, I am now walking in my ministry. I am now a minister of the Gospel of Jesus Christ, and I proclaim His Name gladly! The Lord PULLED ME OUT FOR A PURPOSE!

The Lord restored my life so that I could be a mother to my children and a blessing to my family! God has reconciled my relationship with my children, and it continues to grow stronger. He has put me in a place that I can pray for my family and speak the wisdom of God to them. I know now that the Lord has smiled upon my life, and I am excited to live before my family as an example for Him. I WAS PULLED OUT FOR A PURPOSE!

Furthermore, the Lord has allowed me to graduate from college with a bachelor's degree and two master's degrees. I am also a Licensed Clinical Addiction Specialist, Master Addiction Counselor, Certified Clinical Supervisor, Certified Sex Offenders Treatment Specialist, Certified Anger Management Instructor, Substance Abuse Professional for the NC Department of Transportation, Certified Trauma Specialist, and a Certified Prime for Life Instructor for Alcohol and Drug School. THE LORD HAS PULLED ME OUT FOR A PURPOSE!

The Lord has allowed me to start my own business, form my own nonprofit organization, and chair the outreach ministry for my church. I have gone from having no place to stay to owning my home! Likewise, I have gone from having to ask for a ride to having several of my own vehicles. I have said all of this to say that God has pulled me out of a pitiful state, and He did it for a purpose! I will never forget what the Lord has done for me, and I want to encourage my readers that He will do the same for you! God knows how to pull you out of whatever you are in and bring you into His Divine Purpose! I Praise the Lord!!! I was PULLED OUT FOR A PURPOSE!!!!

CHAPTER 12

Letters to My Children

Making amends to the people you've hurt along the way is very important on the road back from a troubled journey. Here are two letters I wrote and eventually gave to my children early on in my recovery, as a start for reconciliation.

Letter to my son Rodney James Smith (RJ). To my dear son, RJ: I'm writing this letter to share my heart and express my love for you. So much has happened through the years, and I wanted you to know some of the reasons for my actions. I want you to know that through it all, it was never your fault for anything that has ever taken place. When I was pregnant with you, I was addicted to crack cocaine, alcohol, and marijuana. I tried to get help, but I just could not kick the habit. In fact, I went into labor with you at the neighborhood corner store. I have always loved you from the moment I felt you move in my stomach. When I gave birth to you and looked into your big eyes, you melted my heart. There were times I left you because the cravings for the drugs were so strong that I couldn't handle it. I always left you with loving family members like Granddad, Papa, Grandma

Charlotte, and Grandma Ann because I knew that they could give you everything that you needed and surround you with love. I never sent you to live with your grandparents because of your behaviors or anything that you had done. I thought I was making the best decision for you as they could give you stability and a better life. I never wanted you to be in the "hood" because I never wanted you to experience the hell that I was experiencing. You may have felt like I was hard on you, but I know how cruel and mean this world can be. Every action and response I made was for you to have a fighting chance. I wanted you to go forth and be the greatest man that you could be. I'm grateful to God for blessing me with such a loving, caring, and intelligent son. You are a precious gift from God and my heart is made glad because of this. There is nothing I can do to change my past, but I want you to know that I love you dearly son and I'm so very proud of you. Love, Mom

Letter to daughter Alexis Royale Savage (June 2, 1998. I had just given birth to her, and I had to complete my sentence in prison) My dearest Alexis, you took your time coming but you finally made it on May 31, 1998 at 7:30 p.m. I felt all alone but you were with me all the time. God was also there, telling me that he would never leave me or forsake me. I tried walking you down, but you said you wanted to stay here a little while longer. When you finally came, I was so relieved. You were so tiny. You would open your little eyes and look at me. We spent one night together. It broke my heart to leave you. May God be with you till we meet again. Love, Mommy

About The Author

Minister Lorie M. Savage, MA, LCAS, CCS, CSOTS, MAC, SAP Lorie Tyson Savage, a native and resident of Pitt County, NC, was born on March 26, 1973 to Annie Louise Tyson and the late James Teel, Jr. Min. Savage is the proud parent of Rodney James Smith, Alexis Royale Savage and grandmother to King Amari Boyd. After almost losing her life to drugs, Min. Savage gave her life to Christ on February 1, 2002. She is an active member of the Philippi Church of Christ where the pastor is the honorable Dr. Dameion Royal. She is the chairperson of the Outreach Ministry which she holds near and dear to her heart. She also facilitates the "'Fearfully and Wonderfully Made" girls' group, focusing on suicide prevention, trauma, self-esteem, and other teenage issues. Professionally, she has been in the substance abuse and mental health field for 17 years teaching substance abuse prevention to elementary-high school students and providing treatment and recovery to adults of all ages and ethnic groups. Min. Savage also provides therapeutic interventions to children and adolescents through individual and group therapy. Her specialty is working with individuals with serious and persistent mental illnesses, co-occurring disorders and those that are dually diagnosed. She is experienced in intensive in-home treatment providing therapeutic skills to adolescents and their families in the home setting. Min. Savage has also worked as a Reentry Outreach Specialist assisting ex-offenders in finding housing, jobs, obtaining a vocational skill or degree so that they can enter back into society successfully. She also assisted Sherriff Dance with the startup of the WEAR and SHARP program by volunteering to her service to provide group therapy to women and men while incarcerated at the Pitt County Detention Center. She obtained her Bachelor of Arts degree in Psychology from Shaw University, Raleigh, NC, her Master of Counseling from Webster University in Myrtle Beach, South Carolina, and she completed her Master of Christian Ministry from Liberty University, Lynchburg Va. She is currently enrolled in the Doctorate of Traumatology program at Liberty University. Minister Savage is a Licensed Clinical Addiction Specialist, Master Addiction Counselor, Certified Clinical Supervisor, Certified Sex Offender Treatment Specialist, Certified Anger Management Instructor, Certified Prime for Life Instructor for Alcohol and Drug school, Substance Abuse professional for North Carolina Department for Transportation, Founder and former CEO of Starting Pointe, Inc and Founder and Executive Director of Great Things Foundation, I.N.C. (In The Name of Christ). She recently obtained her certification as a Bonafide and Certified GIANT KILLER slaying all demons that would try to keep her, her family, or friends from being all that God has called them to be!!! Min. Savage travels all over eastern North Carolina and surrounding states sharing her testimony and sharing the goodness of Jesus. On June 11th, 2017, she stood behind the sacred desk and delivered her initial sermon entitled, "I'm Advertising for the King" inspired by the scripture Psalm 124. Lorie's ministry has global impact as she has proclaimed the gospel of Jesus Christ to her brothers and sisters in Nairobi, Kenya in Africa. She often states that it has been an honor and a privilege to be called out by Jesus Christ himself to speak life to a dying world. Even though Min. Savage is chosen and not preferred, she is still GOD'S CHOICE!!! Her favorite scripture and motto is Philippians 4:13 - "I can do all things through Christ which strengthen me."

www.ingramcontent.com/pod-product-compliance
Lightning Source LLC
Chambersburg PA
CBHW060352130626
46553CB00003B/1191